You Know You're Surfing The Net Too Much When . . .

AVIV M. ILAN & DAVID ILAN

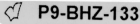

Adams Media Corporation
HOLBROOK, MASSACHUSETTS

Published by
Adams Media Corporation
260 Center Street, Holbrook, MA 02343

ISBN: 1-58062-003-5

Printed in Canada.
J I H G F E D C B A

Library of Congress Cataloging-in-Publication-attached Data
ILAN, AVIV M.
You know you're surfing the net too much when— /
by Aviv M. ILAN and DAVID ILAN.
        p.   cm.
     ISBN 1-58062-003-5
   1. Internet (Computer network)—Humor.
   2. Electronic mail systems—Humor.
      I. ILAN, DAVID. II. Title.
PN6231.I62157   1998
818'.5402—dc21   97-51577
                          CIP

Any trademarks, advertising slogans or cheerful "welcome" greetings are the property of the company that owns them, and we make no claim to ownership or to having originated them. This book should not be used to back up your hard drive. Also, we do not recommend using this book as a mouse pad, surge protector, or fly swatter. This side up.
                                                    —*AVIV M. ILAN and DAVID ILAN, bookathr@.com.*

This book is available at quantity discounts for bulk purchases.
For information, call 1-800-872-5627
(in Massachusetts, 781-767-8100).

Visit our home page at http://www.adamsmedia.com

Address http://surfingthenet.com Links

ACKNOWLEDGMENTS

We would like to thank Ami Ioder and Lital Barkan for their support in writing this book and in all other areas of our lives. We would like to thank Phineas and Anika for their love and affection.

We would also like to thank our agent, Sheree Bykofsky, for her constant efforts on our behalf, and our editor, Ed Walters, and everyone at Adams Media.

To our parents, Jacob
(coffeejoke@aol.com) and
Hava Ilan, who give us so
much and ask for so little.

INTRODUCTION

The Internet, the World Wide Web, the Information Superhighway. The possibilities are endless, the uses are unlimited. Well...maybe for some pathetic newbie. But not for you. You've seen every Web site, you've chatted in every chat room, you've B.S.'d on every BBS.

You were surfing the Net when the superhighway was just an unpaved, one-lane country road. You're the

[v]

original netizen, honorary
mayor of Webville, the stuff
that Net surfing legends are
made of. Generations from
now, kids will gather around
at www.campfire.com and tell
stories of how you first
blazed the trails so people
everywhere could enjoy the
benefits of being connected.

But surfing the Net day
and night, through all kinds
of weather, has its
downfalls. You forgot how to
walk. Your hand is frozen in
the shape of a claw. The

vi

lining of your throat has turned to sandpaper.

Your doctor, your lawyer, your neighbors, even the phone company told you to cut back on your online time. But it wasn't until you posted the question to your friends on your favorite newsgroup, and all one hundred thousand of them said the same thing, did the message finally hit home. You need to unplug.

This book is the perfect tool to help you access your normal life again. By picking

up this book and not waiting
for the online version,
you've shown that there is a
light at the end of the
tunnel, and it is not coming
from the glow of your
computer screen.

Now comes the hardest
part, flipping the pages
without a mouse, going
through life without a Net.
Because in the real world,
the offline world, there is
no "back" button.

Instant messages
take too long.

1

You carry JPEGs
of your loved ones
in your wallet.

2

You lost your
virginity online.

3

For your honeymoon,
you went to
www.thecaribbean.com

4

The only time you leave the house is to buy a new keyboard.

You've worn out yet another one of those rubber balls inside your mouse.

b

You have ASDF
and JKL; permanently
imprinted on your
fingertips.

You think of
having sex as
"plug and play."

The only time you
see the sun is on
the solar livecam. ⌖

9

You actually say
"laughing out loud"
instead of laughing.

Bill Gates returns
your e-mail first.

The last time you
used snail-mail the
post office was
using ponies.

The sound of modems
connecting gets you
in the mood.

The doctor told you
to lose weight,
so you joined
alt.recreation.users.gym

14

You make popcorn
and reload images
all night.

The sweetest words
you've ever heard are
"you've got mail."

You have more names
in your online
address book than the
Montana White Pages.

You e-mail your
spouse good night.

18

When you're coming
down with a cold,
you eat the
Norton antivirus
installation disk.

You take pills
to control your
emoticons.

Your kids are
sad and you tell
them, "Turn that
open parentheses
upside down."

Asked how you're
doing, your
auto-responder
replies, "Fine.
And yourself?"

During a blackout,
you unplugged the
generator from
your grandfather's
life-support system
to stay connected.

You spend half your
day reading e-mail
and the other half
responding to it.

Your computer
runs faster than
your car.

25

You laugh at people
who still refer to
it as a period.

You need a Rolodex
to keep track of all
your Bookmarks.

You put on a wet
suit and fins before
logging on.

28

You think AOL's
new pricing plan is
like a gift sent
from the heavens.

You rooted for Big
Blue in the chess
championships.

You believe your
breakfast sausage is
merely a link to
your eggs.

31

You consider
30 minutes of live
chat with your kids
as quality time.

Your server
went down and you
ate your own foot
to survive.

You don't go
to the bathroom,
you download.

You refer to
your den as your
chat room.

You don't need
help from your
kids to set up
parental control.

36

You're convinced
that Arnold
Schwarzenegger said,
"Alta Vista, baby."

You refer to
childbirth as a
self-extracting
archive.

The only time you
use your voice is
when talking to
technical support.

You have a wall
hanging that reads,
"Homepage Sweet
Homepage."

You believe the
world is divided
into two types
of people...clients
and servers.

You require people
to log on before
entering your house.

42

Unzipping files
turns you on.

You have a bumper
sticker on your
modem that says,
"Born to Be Baud."

You alphabetize
according to
the QWERTY
keyboard layout.

Your mousepad has
skid marks.

You adopted
two miles of the
Information
Superhighway.

You have a T-shirt
that says, "So many
Web sites...so
little time."

You wore out
the "@" button on
your keyboard.

You put the "F"
in RTFM.

50

You invite the neighbors over to watch QuickTime movies of your family vacations.

Streetlights flicker
when you boot up
your system.

52

You keep trying to
minimize your boss.

Your Web page gets
more hits than Mike
Tyson's punching bag.

Your eyeballs
are square.

You refer to
hand-me-downs
as "shareware."

You don't sleep,
you shut down.

Your big screen
projection monitor
covers the
entire wall.

You're a
volunteer member
of SCERD (System
Crash Emergency
Rescue Detail).

You know your weight
in kilobytes.

You remind your
online lovers that
it's not the speed
of your modem, it's
how you use it.

61

You wear a dust cover to bed.

You wear a ribbon to show your support in the fight against computer viruses.

You consider
The Net a classic
masterpiece of the
American cinema.

You feel that
HAL 9000 was deeply
misunderstood.

You wrote
Stephen King a
ten-page synopsis
of technical
inaccuracies in
The Lawnmower Man.

You have your own
MCI representative.

You have
webbed feet.

68

Yahoo asks for
your help with
difficult searches.

Ninety-nine out of 100 times, URouLette sends you to a site you've already seen.

You've trained
your dog to fetch
new postings to
your newsgroups.

You run to the store
for a gallon of milk
and more megs.

You shave in front
of a mirror page.

You need a password
to open your
refrigerator.

74

Eventually, all
links lead back
to you.

75

People
affectionately call
you the Dick Clark
of the Internet
Relay Chats.

Worldwide is a
little too limited
for you.

77

You think of
your brain as a
slow but necessary
search engine.

You wrote the book
*Around the World in
Eighty Clicks.*

You were a technical
advisor on the set
of *War Games*.

You refuse to eat
at any restaurant
not featuring
dropdown menus.

Instead of reaching
for something, you
try to drag your
arrow to it.

You've designed
a full-body workout
you can do while
sitting at
your desk.

83

You don't swear, you
use hypertext.

You were asking it
before it was
a FAQ.

Half the Internet
community knows you
as the Big Kahuna.

The other half knows
you as Gidget.

87

You brought in a
truckload of sand
and some sea gulls
to make the
experience complete.

The only music CDs
you own are by the
Beach Boys.

Your driver's license
has your screen
name and e-mail
address on it.

90

You can create a
full-scale detailed
map of Rhode Island
using only the
"@" key.

You have four
separate phone
lines, yet you
live alone.

92

You're the online
Twister champion.

America Online
solved all its
access problems by
kicking you off.

The stewardess
has to pry away
your laptop from you
so they can land
the plane.

You see the world
in ten frames
per second.

You're a veteran
of several
international
flame wars.

You need hours of
therapy when a host
refuses connection.

Even your abacus
is hooked up to
a modem.

You haven't gotten a
phone bill in three
months because
you're still on the
same call.

You really do
have a mouse in
your pocket.

You adopted
"Surfin' Safari" as
your theme song.

You've been married
two years, yet you've
never met in person.

You dream in
encrypted code.

Your Usenet group
moderator was the
best man at your
wedding.

You give your kids
online time as a
weekly allowance.

You think WebTV
is the greatest
combination since
peanut butter
and jelly.

You have a low-grade,
year-round tan
from the glow of
the screen.

You get in a cab and
give the driver your
Web address.

Your fingers are
worn down to
little nubs.

You anxiously await
the expansion to the
Universe Wide Web.

You remember when
Net addresses only
needed two W's.

Your kids come back
from college and you
ask them, "Where
have you been?"

To speed up the
downloading process,
you've routed your
modem through
your microwave.

You wouldn't know you
were dead unless
you read it in the
online obituaries.

115

You get seven new e-mails while reading your morning e-mails.

You've downloaded
every possible file.

117

You tell your grandkids that when you were little, you had to connect using a rotary phone.

You order a pizza
online and then print
it out on scratch-
and-sniff paper.

119

You added another surge protector so you can plug in the mini-fridge.

You start off all
your speeches with,
"My fellow netizens."

You bump into an
old friend on the
street and run home
so you both can
live chat.

122

Your husband threatens
to leave you, so you
agree to join a
marriage counseling
Usenet group. ⇖

123

Your wife
complains she feels
disconnected, so you
surprise her with
her own account.

You take your
computer along
on dates.

125

You refer to your
computer as your
better half.

You log on to the
weather homepage
instead of looking
out the window.

You produced the *Retiring on $19.95 a Month* infomercial.

You wax your
motherboard.

Your first modem
ran at 1 bps.

You reminisce about
playing *Pong* over
the Internet.

You've replaced your right eye with a small video camera.

132

You think the
missing link is an
online treasure hunt.

You don't go to
Internet cafés for
the coffee.

You took the wheels
off of your computer
chair and put them
on your fridge.

Your computer desk
comes equipped with
all the supplies
needed to survive
a major catastrophe.

136